Unleashing Facebook Visibility

A comprehensive guide to boosting your online presence (*no pink hair required*)

Heather Rose

Copyright © 2023 by Heather Rose.

All rights reserved. No part of this book may be used or reproduced in any form whatsoever without written permission except in the case of brief quotations in critical articles or reviews.

Printed by Amazon

For more information about Pink Fizz Social :

Website :   https://pinkfizz.social
Email :   info@pinkfizz.social

Cover Design : Khatoon B (fiverr account 'fashionerstudio)

ISBN :   9798860433366

Second Edition: October 2023

Dedication
To Barry and Isaac, my superheroes

CONTENTS

- CONTENTS 1
- FORWARD 8
- **UNLOCKING THE POWER OF FACEBOOK FOR YOUR BUSINESS** 9
  - UNVEILING THE POWER OF FACEBOOK 9
- **LAYING THE FOUNDATION: YOUR BUSINESS AND FACEBOOK** 14
  - COMBATING CONSUMER MISTRUST 15
  - OTHER INFLUENCING FACTORS 16
  - HOW MUCH YOU INTERACT (BEING SOCIAL) 19
  - GIVING VALUE 20
  - SHORT FORM VIDEO CONTENT 21
- **DECODING FACEBOOK'S ALGORITHM: THE KEY TO VISIBILITY** 23
  - DO YOU HAVE AN IDEAL CLIENT AVATAR? 23
  - ENGAGE WITH YOUR AUDIENCE 24
  - GIVE VALUE AND THEN SOME MORE 24
  - ENGAGE ON OTHER POSTS 26
  - POST AT THE RIGHT TIMES 27
  - DON'T GET INTO TROUBLE (FACEBOOK JAIL) 28
  - DON'T OVER POST 30
  - WAKE UP YOUR SOCIALS 30
  - KEEP IT SHORT AND SWEET 31
- **OPTIMISING YOUR PROFILE** 32
  - GETTING YOUR PROFILE RIGHT 32
  - HOW DO YOU USE YOUR PERSONAL PROFILE? 34
- **OPTIMISING YOUR BUSINESS PAGE** 37
  - CONTENT ADVICE: WHAT TO POST 38
  - SETTING UP YOUR PAGE FOR SUCCESS 39

Unleashing Facebook Visibility

THE POWER OF FACEBOOK GROUPS 41
SETTING UP YOUR FACEBOOK GROUP 42
SO NOW LET'S TALK CONTENT 46
HOW OFTEN SHOULD YOU POST IN YOUR GROUP? 49

CONTENT FOUNDATIONS: THE FIVE PILLARS TO CAPTURE ATTENTION 50
FIVE PILLARS OF CONTENT 50

SPINNING SUCCESS: CRAFTING YOUR CONTENT WHEEL 56
HERE'S HOW TO CREATE A CONTENT WHEEL 56
EXAMPLE OF MY CONTENT WHEEL 57
BENEFITS OF THE CONTENT WHEEL 57

CONTENT THAT CONVERTS: NAVIGATING YOUR BUYER'S JOURNEY 61
STAGE 1: AWARENESS 61
STAGE 2: CONSIDERATION 62
STAGE 3: DECISION 62

HOOKLINES & CTAS: CAPTIVATE AND COMPEL 66
HOOKLINES: THE SPARK THAT IGNITES ENGAGEMENT 66
SO, WHAT EXACTLY IS A HOOKLINE? 66
WHY ARE HOOKLINES SO CRUCIAL? 66
CTAS: THE COMPASS OF ENGAGEMENT 68
THE DYNAMIC DUO 70

THE ART OF STORYTELLING: BUILDING BONDS THROUGH CONNECTION 72
THE POWER OF STORYTELLING: FORGING BONDS THAT LAST 72
YOUR NARRATIVE, YOUR LEGACY 77

EMBRACING AUTHENTICITY: FORGING GENUINE CONNECTIONS 78
THE POWER OF PERSONAL CONNECTION: GOING BEYOND PRODUCTS 78

DATA SPEAKS: THE INFLUENCE OF PERSONAL STORIES 78
EMBRACING VULNERABILITY: SEAMLESSLY INFUSING PERSONAL STORIES . 79
CRAFTING BONDS THROUGH AUTHENTICITY 83

ELEVATE YOUR AUDIENCE: THE POWER OF HELPING 84
THE PSYCHOLOGY OF HELP: NURTURING TRUST AND CONNECTION 84
ADVANCING BY ASSISTANCE 88

VALUE BEYOND MEASURE: BUILDING LASTING RELATIONSHIPS 89
VALUE-DRIVEN CONTENT: THE PSYCHOLOGY OF TRUST AND CONNECTION 89
THE PATH TO CONNECTION AND GROWTH 93

CELEBRATE AND CONNECT: NURTURING RELATIONSHIPS THROUGH SHARED JOY 94
CELEBRATION DAYS AND THE BUYER'S JOURNEY 96

UNLEASH YOUR FACEBOOK VISIBILITY JOURNEY 101

THE ACADEMY 103

ABOUT THE AUTHOR 104

ACKNOWLEDGMENTS 106

APPENDIX 1 108

TABLE OF ABBREVIATIONS 108

YOUR NOTES 109

Forward

This book is for anyone who struggles with self-doubt, lack of confidence, fear of visibility, and those who want success but don't know how to get it.

I'm here to let you know you can do it, and I have faith in you, even if we don't know each other.

That's just how I feel.

Everyone can be whoever they want, anyone can succeed in whatever they choose.

Sending this one out to all my bullies.

You said I wouldn't be anything. I was worthless, fat, ugly, and stupid. That I should kill myself. I owe you all thanks; your cruelty drove me to prove you wrong.

Who's laughing now?

Ok let's crack on to what you're here for...

How to become more visible on Facebook

CHAPTER 1

Unlocking The Power Of Facebook For Your Business

In this chapter, we're about to embark on an exploration of Facebook's potential and the tremendous impact it can have on your business.

Join me as we delve into the realm of Facebook's capabilities, unravelling the layers that make it a game-changer for establishing a robust online presence.

I'll share my experiences and tips on how to make a successful business on this platform.

Facebook's Integral Role in Our Lives
Facebook has woven itself intricately into the fabric of our daily existence. It's more than just a social media platform; it's a dynamic hub where people connect, share, and engage.

The scope of Facebook's influence on modern communication is staggering.

Unveiling the Power of Facebook
Let's start by shedding light on some remarkable facts about Facebook:

Statistics valid at time of publication

Unleashing Facebook Visibility

- With an impressive 60.6% share of all social media users, Facebook stands as the reigning champion of the social media landscape
- A staggering 3 billion individuals engage with Facebook on a monthly basis, representing an astonishing global reach
- Each day witnesses 1.7 billion active users, a testament to Facebook's unmatched popularity
- The platform has around 1.8 billion actively used groups every month, which is remarkable considering it has 10 million groups
- Facebook is an important business tool with 200 million business pages hosted globally
- Every day, 1.25 billion Facebook users watch around 1 billion hours of video content.
- The prominence of Facebook Live is undeniable, generating a whopping 1 million daily views
- The average user dedicates approximately 19.5 hours per month to the platform

Seizing Opportunities and Benefits
The statistics alone paint a vivid picture of the opportunities that lie within Facebook's realm for business owners. The potential for growth, engagement, and connection is immense, creating a treasure trove of possibilities.

The Unparalleled Reach
One of Facebook's most distinctive features is its colossal reach. With billions of users worldwide, businesses have an unparalleled opportunity to connect with a global audience.

This far-reaching potential allows brands to expand their visibility and establish a presence on an unprecedented scale.

Laser-Sharp Targeting
Facebook's precision in targeting is a game-changer. Business owners can tailor their content to reach specific demographics, interests, and behaviours. By crafting ads that resonate with distinct groups, businesses can start conversations with the right audience.

While paid advertising is a viable route, my personal success story illustrates that organic growth is very achievable through dedicated effort.

Brand Building and Recognition
A well-crafted Facebook business page serves as an online showcase for products, services, and brand values. With engaging content, business owners can captivate their audience, reinforcing brand identity and fostering brand loyalty.

Throughout this book, we will delve into the art of optimising Facebook business pages and groups to enhance brand recognition.

Cultivating Engagement and Community
Facebook's unparalleled strength lies in its ability to foster community and engagement. The platform thrives on connectivity, with groups serving as virtual meeting places for like-minded individuals. This unique feature provides an avenue for businesses to share captivating content, start

conversations, and cultivate a sense of belonging within their audience.

Insights and Informed Decision

Metrics and analytics are the lifeblood of effective marketing. Facebook's analytics empower entrepreneurs to comprehend audience interactions with their content.

Armed with this invaluable insight, businesses can refine their strategies, fine-tune targeting efforts, and make data-driven decisions to enhance both marketing initiatives and overall business performance.

Social Proof and Trust

The power of social proof cannot be overstated. On Facebook, customers have the ability to leave reviews and recommendations for businesses.

Positive feedback and recommendations from others bolster a business's credibility and trustworthiness, transforming a mere business entity into a trustworthy brand.

As we continue our journey through this book, you'll discover practical strategies, real-world examples from UK businesses, and actionable steps to harness the full potential of Facebook for your business.

Through a comprehensive understanding of Facebook's capabilities, you'll be equipped to navigate the dynamic landscape of social media with confidence.

Whether you're looking to strengthen brand identity, foster engagement, or drive sales, Facebook offers the tools and resources to realise your business goals.

CHAPTER 2

Laying The Foundation: Your Business and Facebook

In this chapter, we are going to talk about how Facebook scores you.

Yep, you have heard it right. Facebook scores you on what you do on the platform and rewards you accordingly - known as *The Algorithm*.

I really dislike the terminology — algorithm — and how the word is banded about on social media. Yes, social media is run on algorithms, but "beating the algorithm" is impossible. However, we can work with it.

> *Secret: The Biggest Algorithm That There Is, Is YOU!*

You're the most valuable asset to your business. Your business is unique because of you and what you bring to the table. The rapport will be built with you; the know, like, and trust factor. Therefore, the biggest asset to your business is you, so be your own algorithm. The key tip I give to clients is to be authentic and show up as yourself on social media. That's what will make you relatable to your audience, so don't be afraid to be you!

Combating Consumer Mistrust

So, on Facebook, we've seen a lot of fake news, spam, and fake accounts in recent years. It made users feel insecure and unsafe on the platform. Recently, Facebook has been working hard to ensure the safety of its users by paying closer attention to the content being posted.

If I post on Facebook today, just a small fraction of my followers will see it. Why? Facebook's just testing if my content is interesting and if people will engage with it. So, Facebook is keeping my audience safe.

If my post gets shared, interactions (likes, loves, etc.) and comments, Facebook knows its users want to see my content. It will then push it out to another small percentage of people and test the waters again, and the process is repeated.

Facebook uses various algorithms to score the content on its platform to determine visibility and reach. The specifics about the algorithms are top secret, but there are things that influence the rating and reward of content.

Engagement
As mentioned above, Facebook likes content that gets people talking — the more likes, comments, and shares, the better. So, if your content sparks meaningful conversations, it'll get more views.

Relevance
Facebook's goal is to show you relevant content. The algorithm considers your past actions, likes, and

15

conversations to judge if a piece of content is worthy to show you.

Authenticity and Quality
Facebook prioritises authentic and high-quality content. Posts that violate community standards or contain misleading information may receive lower scores. You may also be penalised by your account being put into Facebook jail, limited reach, etc.

Consistency
Regularly posting relevant and engaging content can contribute to better visibility. Consistency in posting can help build an audience and increases the likelihood of content being rewarded. Facebook wants to keep its audience engaged, so if you are being consistent, you will be rewarded.

Other Influencing Factors
I would now like to go on and share some other ways that Facebook score you. I'm going to list these in simple terms, giving you actionable steps that you can take away and implement immediately.

Stories
Using the story feature on Facebook can get you huge visibility and reach a wider audience. Stories appear prominently at the top of the Facebook news feed and are displayed for 24 hours.

75% of users now scroll through their stories and reel feed before scrolling through an actual newsfeed!

If you are not utilising this feature consistently, you are missing a trick.

Stories allow businesses to share content in a more interactive and engaging format. Allowing you to capture the attention of your audience.

Try using:

- images
- videos
- stickers
- filters
- run polls
- ask questions
- countdowns

Audience members can interact with you and take action, like visiting your website or having conversations. They enable you to share your brand story in a captivating and concise manner.

You can share:

- snippets of customer testimonials
- product launches
- events
- lead magnets
- course/masterclasses
- behind-the-scenes footage

Unleashing Facebook Visibility

You can have a glorious mix of personal and business content, which helps build the trust and like factor with your audience.

EMOJI'S
This is another feature that Facebook wants you to utilise.

It wasn't that Mark Zuckerberg was drunk in the pub with his mates one night and said, "come on lads, let's bring out some emojis just for the laugh."

Nope, he brought them out for a reason. Emojis make text pop! 🔥 They highlight important words and make things look more appealing. 😎 Emojis also adds an extra layer of meaning and emotion to a text-based communication. They help show your tone, intent, and feelings in a quick and visual way, which makes your message more interesting and easier to connect with.

Emojis have also been shown to increase engagement rates in online communications. Adding emojis to your posts, emails, or chats can help you connect with your customers and followers 🤝, get conversations going 💬, and build a sense of community 🌼.

Happy Birthday Feature
We all receive notifications when one of our friends has a birthday. Guess what? Facebook sends you this notification for a reason: to use it.

Using this feature can be beneficial for business owners as it helps build customer relationships. Acknowledging customers' birthdays by sending appropriate messages helps foster a personal connection.

You can make your followers feel valued by sending them birthday wishes. It's a 'hance to connect with them, communicate, and encourage engagement. Remember, comments and direct messages can lead to business opportunities. Plus, responding to birthday notifications is a great way to build your engagement score and increase your visibility (see influencing factors above).

How Much You Interact (Being Social)
I see so many business owners just post and run, i.e. putting a post out but not commenting on others' posts. Then complain about lack of engagement and low conversion rates!

Reaching out to your audience on Facebook helps establish a connection. Take part in discussions, respond to comments and messages; it will make your brand more human.

Your personal presence on Facebook adds authenticity and credibility to your business.

It shows that there is a real person behind the brand who is actively involved and invested in the community. This transparency can foster trust and loyalty among your audience.

Share your industry knowledge and tips to establish yourself as an expert. By being active on Facebook, you can prove your expertise, establish trust, and draw in customers who respect your knowledge. Besides, who else can share and promote your businesses content more effectively than you? Share updates, blog posts, product announcements, new launches, and customer testimonials with your network. It'll help grow your audience.

Remember to balance personal and professional interactions on Facebook. People need to see the real you as well. This enables you to build the know, like, and trust factor with your audience and become relatable. So behind-the-scenes and personal life content are just as important to share.

Giving Value

This is another area Facebook will look at and reward you accordingly. Facebook wants to keep users happy, so it shows them interesting things they'll love. Great content that offers value enhances overall experience on the platform. Facebook wants users to stay active and engaged on its platform. By showcasing great content, it can keep users entertained, informed, and connected. From a business standpoint, this leads to increased user retention and higher engagement rates.

Providing value through your content is crucial for gaining your audience's trust and loyalty. People will love it if you give them helpful tips, interesting perspectives, or fun content. It's all about getting noticed and shared, and interesting content does just that. Your audience will share your content if they find it valuable. This can get you more visibility and reach new audiences.

Short Form Video Content

85% of users now watch video footage — lives and reels — more than any other content. If you're not using this format, you're missing out on sales and falling behind. Short form video content is only going to get bigger!

Video Footage Provides a Powerful Medium for Storytelling.

With short form videos, businesses can easily tell their story, show what they offer, and make an emotional connection. This can create a memorable and impactful brand experience for viewers.

Short videos have the potential to go viral and spread rapidly across social networks. If the content is interesting, entertaining, or informative, it can generate a huge buzz. Posting a viral video can attract a whole new audience and skyrocket your brand's visibility and business potential.

Short videos work well to show product features, how-tos, tips, hacks, or quick tutorials. Businesses can showcase benefits, solve customer problems, and build trust. While also showcasing your personality, which will help you become relatable to your audience.

Unleashing Facebook Visibility

You can find more training on the above within my courses and workshops. Please visit https://pinkfizz.social.

CHAPTER 3

Decoding Facebook's Algorithm: The Key To Visibility

To nail your Facebook strategy, you need to know who you're talking to.

Do You Have an Ideal Client Avatar?
Knowing your ideal client is key to understanding who you're talking to and who your message is for. It is about understanding your clients' demographics, interests, frustrations and online behaviours.

This knowledge will help you tailor your content specifically. Your messaging will resonate with your specific audience and increase the chances of engagement and sales. This will also make your content writing so much easier too, as you will clearly understand who it is directed at and whom you are talking to.

For more in-depth training on niching – check out my course: *Niching to Increase Your Sales.*

https://pinkfizz.social/product/niching-to-increase-your-sales/

Engage With Your Audience

To prove you care about their opinions and questions, respond promptly to comments, messages, and mentions. You want to create a community and earn loyalty; asking questions, engaging followers, and interacting with them does this.

> *Remember, Facebook loves conversations.*

One of things I always ask my clients if they say that their Facebook is like tumbleweed is 'Are you giving love?'

Give love to get love back. You need to interact with others if you want engagement on your posts. If you're not engaging, Facebook won't show your content. The platform needs you to be active in it.

Give Value and Then Some More

To add value, take time to know your audience — what they like, need, want, and struggle with. To do this, it's crucial to understand who your ideal client is. Make up an ideal client (you can even give them a name) and write your content like you're talking to them. This technique will make your content writing so much easier.

Guess what else can help you know your audience better? Ask them! Engage in conversations, run polls, and learn what content they need.

Teach your audience with your content using the five pillars. I'll cover the five content pillars later. Post articles, blogs, newsletters, how-tos, tutorials, insights and tricks.

Share exclusive content with your audience that they won't find anywhere else. This could include behind-the-scenes looks, sneak peeks, or early access to things. It'll make them feel like VIPs for following you.

Don't forget to reply to comments, messages and posts to stay engaged with your audience. Encourage discussions, ask questions and create a sense of community. Everyone wants to belong and feel like they're part of something. Building communities is what Facebook is all about.

Want more engagement on your posts? Use visuals like bright images, pics with faces, and text overlays on graphics, videos, infographics, and memes. Pictures and videos get noticed and improve your message.

Stay update to date with latest trends, news and developments in your industry or niche. Share updates with your audience to keep them informed. You'll become a respected authority in your field because of your knowledge.

The key to giving value is being real with your audience, gaining their trust, and connecting with them. Don't be afraid to share personal stories or behind-the-scenes moments. It'll foster a genuine connection and show who you are as a person. Remember, people by from people so show the face behind the business.

Engage on Other Posts

I always say to my clients you must give love to get love back.

You won't get a lot of comments and likes if you don't comment and like other people's posts. You're putting stuff out and crossing your fingers for interaction. Then you disappear from Facebook until your next share.

I call this type of activity *post and run,* it is a sure-fire way to alienate your audience rather than engage them.

Don't just leave, explore other people's content. Taking part in conversations helps you build connections and reach more people. Leave thoughtful comments when engaging with others' posts and add value to the conversation. End your comment with a question whenever you can. This gets the person to reply and starts a conversation. It's a sure-fire way to make connections and Facebook will notice your efforts. Leave comments that are at least four words long, so Facebook doesn't think you're a bot.

If you talk to others, you'll become an authority in your field. Show off your expertise and people will trust you and come to you for help. Liking and commenting on other posts helps you connect with potential customers and influencers, too. You might make some great connections and find new opportunities.

And remember, always reply to comments on your own posts. It says you appreciate their feedback, you're glad they are engaged with your content, and it inspires them to keep interacting.

Post at the Right Times

Posting your content at the right time is crucial for many reasons.

To maximise your chances of getting engagement on Facebook, make sure you're posting when your audience is most likely to be online and scrolling. Otherwise, your content could easily get buried and forgotten thanks to the algorithm.

Speaking of Facebook's algorithm, the timing and engagement of your posts matter. If it gets lots of likes and comments right away, Facebook thinks it's good stuff and shows it to more people.

Your insights can help you determine when to post for maximum engagement. If you have over 50 members in your Facebook group, you can find insights in the settings. The charts show when your group is most active each day.

For business pages, I recommend using Facebook's own scheduling tool as it suggests an optimum day and time to post.

Don't Get Into Trouble (Facebook Jail)

There are many activities that can get your account down-ranked, restricted, suspended, or cancelled. We affectionately call this being put into Facebook jail. The punishment depends on your crime or suspected crime. Sounds ridiculous, right? Sadly, it happens all the time.

This is quite a big topic, and many fall foul of Facebook's restrictions purely down to unaware. Although you may never be 100 per cent certain of the reason for Facebook's penalty, I will share a few of the common ones with you.

- Using Third Party Apps (e.g. Hootsuite, Later, Buffer, Sprout Social, Post Planner, SocialBee, Canva, Social Champ,)

  Facebook wants you to make use of it's in-house scheduling tools. You can schedule posts directly in your groups and business pages. Meta Business Suite was created for you to schedule all your Facebook content from one place.

- External Links
  Facebook wants to keep users on its platform, so using any links in your posts which take people away will down-rank the content. Try to put external links in the comments rather in the body of your posts.

- Trigger Words

Facebook has a long list of words and phrases that it down-ranks posts for. For instance, words like fat loss, diet, comment, link, price, sale, competition, join, sign up, free, cost, and discount, and so on. Facebook will penalise you by reducing your reach, so try making them look different to avoid getting flagged. For instance, L.I.N.K / F-R-E-E

- Hate speech, harassment, or inappropriate content. You probably already know this. Hate speech insults someone's race, religion, ethnicity, gender, sexual orientation, or other protected characteristics. Harassment can be a never-ending stream of unwanted attention, like cyberstalking, threats, or intimidation. Explicit, pornographic, or violent material are inappropriate.

- Robot behaviour
Copying and pasting all over Facebook in different groups or pages triggers Facebook's bot warnings. Even replying to comments, scrolling too fast, or liking too many posts in your newsfeed at once can flag up robotic behaviour.

I've only just scraped the surface here.

You may need a cuppa or something stronger now. Lol!

Unleashing Facebook Visibility

Don't Over Post
Gone are the days of putting out numerous posts a day.

Bombarding your audience with excessive posts can lead to audience fatigue. Yes, it is a thing. Audience fatigue can leave your followers feeling overwhelmed — they may even start to unfollow you!

It is more important to prioritise the quality of your content over quantity. You will have a better chance of capturing your audience's attention and getting them to engage.

Don't go overboard with posts on Facebook, it'll think you're spamming and penalise your account.

I recommend the following guidelines to my clients:

- Personal Profile - 1-3 times a day
- Facebook group - 3 times daily with suitable gaps
- Business Page – once a day

(this does not include paid ads)

Wake Up Your Socials
To kick off your day, I recommend scrolling and commenting on other people's posts, stories, and reels for 10-20 mins before posting anything yourself. Go and share some love. And then post.

This will get your socials going and the algorithm will give your post more visibility.

Top Tip
When sharing love on your stories, the first ones you see in your feed are people that you regularly interact with. Keep scrolling until you find people you haven't talked to in a while and who could be your perfect client. Then, show them some love. Yep, thank me later. Lol.

Keep It Short and Sweet
Short posts get more attention. In today's social media world, people don't have time for long posts. Research shows 101-250 character posts get more engagement.

CHAPTER 4

Optimising Your Profile

Your Facebook profile is like a coffee shop, where people go to check you out and see the face behind the business. This is where you'll build a relationship with your audience.

Remember the know-like-trust factor. Make the most of your Facebook profile for your business. You can establish relationships with potential customers, peers, and influencers by building connections.

Ensure that your personal profile is optimised to begin with.

Getting Your Profile Right

Do you have a clear and professional photo of yourself as your profile photo?

Is your bio effective?

You get 101 characters to write a bio. Make sure it highlights your expertise, and use keywords that your ideal client may search for. These two steps will help create a positive first impression and build trust with potential customers.

You also have an option of having a cover image at the top of your profile. Use this space wisely. I recommend using your cover image in your Customer Relationship Management (CRM) funnel.

How Do I Utilise My Profile Cover Image?

My cover image guides people to my free Facebook Group. Whip up an image (I prefer Canva) with the text "Click to join my group!" When someone clicks the image, it opens the viewing pane where they will see the link to join my group in the comments box.

I'm always looking for ways to grow my group. Change this picture frequently and use it to promote new lead magnets, courses, masterclasses, new launches, and whatever else you want.

Other Details

Have you added your business to your workplace? Tag your business page for a smooth customer journey. Remember to include your contact details and social media links.

Privacy Setting

Finally, I would always suggest that if you're wanting to grow your business using Facebook that you set your personal profile to public.

It's important for potential customers to see your details and content easily. This helps them to know if you're the one they want to connect with.

Public profiles and posts appear higher in search engine results. This makes it much easier for people to find your business when someone looks you up or your related keywords. When you post publicly, more people can see it because others can share it. But I get it, not everyone wants everything public. Facebook allows you can change the privacy of each post; public, friends, friends except... or just a specific list.

How Do You Use Your Personal Profile?

Your Facebook profile can be a great way to market your business. You can make connections with customers, establish your professional brand, and improve your online presence. You can really connect with people, show your expertise, and engage your audience.

To build meaningful connections, you need to engage with your audience actively. Remember to comment, message, and share their posts. Thank your audience for commenting, encourage discussions about your posts. When we're genuine, people stick around, trust us, and spread the word.

Don't be afraid to get personal with your audience. People like hearing about your life, stories, and experiences. It makes them feel like they know you better and can trust you more.

Business Owners Be Wary!

Selling on your personal Facebook profile can get you in trouble, so be careful. I've seen people get their accounts closed without warning and lose everything. Yes, mention your business on your profile, but be clever and sell without selling.

Here are some ideas for you:

Updates and Announcements
Spread the word about your business! Let people know about new launches, upcoming events, and projects you're working on to get them excited.

Share Behind-the-Scenes Insights
Giving glimpses of your business and life strengthens your bond with the audience. Seeing something new is exciting for everyone. Pop culture wouldn't be complete without reality TV. People love to see unvarnished, behind-the-scenes action. You're living in your own reality TV show.

News and Trends
Share insightful articles, studies, facts, myths, etc. Position yourself as a leader and expert in your field of genius.

Tips and How-to Guides
Share helpful tips, tutorials, and guides about your products or services. This shows you know your stuff.

Customer Testimonials and Success Stories
Reviews easily showcase people's positive experiences — this is social proof. Success stories and testimonials help build trust and make people want to buy from or work with you.

Talk About Your Facebook Community
If you have a Facebook group, chat about what's going on in there.

For example:

- You'll be sharing your expertise in a free masterclass on [topic].
- You're going to spill the beans on how to solve [problem].
- We're lucky to have guest expert [name] giving a free talk on [topic].

Feel free to talk about your groups on your Facebook profile. Community is Facebook's buzz word. This means that the algorithm will push your posts out to more people, increasing your reach. Posting regularly about your group will help it grow by bringing more people in.

Remember
Don't just use your personal profiles to promote your business.

Facebook says personal profiles shouldn't *only* be used for business.

Too many blatantly business posts will attract the wrong attention and you could end up in Facebook jail.

CHAPTER 5

Optimising Your Business Page

Your Facebook business page is your virtual shop window. Your business page is somewhere people can come and have a browse around to see what you offer without commitment. It's like having a shop on a busy street where people can drop by anytime without feeling obligated to buy anything.

Or think of it like a business directory. This is where your audience can easily find you. They will see your contact info, what you offer, and get a first impression of you and your business.

It's crucial for entrepreneurs to connect with their audience and build a brand, and having a business page can help. Put your products and services on display, interact with customers, and expand your reach.

You can also use the page analytics to find out about your audience. You can see their age, sex, and demographics, trends, what they like and what content they're into. From there, you can tweak your content, post at optimal times, and market more strategically to increase engagement and reach. You can also use the analytics to see if your ads are working if you choose this option.

But wait for it, only 3% of your followers and likers will see what you post. Why? Facebook gives priority to posts from paying pages, of course. Remember, Facebook is a business just like me and you, and this is how they make their money.

But if you really optimise your page and play the game, you can get a bit more reach. The trick to Facebook pages is posting content that people want to share and engage with.

But how do you do this?

Content Advice: What to Post
My go-to is the 4:1 rule, it never fails, and it's what I recommend to all my clients. Four days of diverse content, including memes, bloopers, quotes, statistics, did you know facts, fun facts, and audience engagement. These posts can get your audience to share or comment, and on the fifth day, drop a sales post.

The only thing that would make an exception to this rule is if your post goes viral or gets a lot of engagement. I'd wait for a good three hours or more and then put up a sales post.

If you create content that gets people interacting and sharing on Facebook, it's going to reward you. You won't have to pay for ads to get your content to a bigger audience.

Paid Ads Can Be Highly Beneficial for Your Business
With Facebook's advanced targeting, you can reach the exact people you want based on their demographics, interests and more. They also help you increase your brands visibility and exposure to a wider audience.

However, (yep another but), you need the funds behind you to make them a success. I wouldn't spend money on ads unless you have a solid marketing budget, and even then, it's not a sure thing. So be ready to cut your losses if it doesn't pan out.

Think of your first few attempts with paid ads as a trial period.

I highly recommend getting a Facebook ads expert to guide you through this investment. It'll make all the difference. This is not my forte, but I know someone who's a total rockstar in this field. If you're interested, please check out Katie Colella - @KatieColellasocial or visit katiecolellasocial.co.uk.

Setting Up Your Page for Success

Your Page's profile needs to be complete and attractive. Use a good quality photo of yourself, not a logo. People want to know who they're connecting with.

Make sure your cover image is clear and eye-catching and reflects your brand and offerings. This is where you could include your logo. Don't forget to advertise your website or social media in this space, just like your personal profile. For example, your banner could guide them to join your Facebook group, visit your website, or grab a free lead magnet. Make all your marketing work for you.

Craft an interesting "About" section, clearly communicating your unique value, mission and offerings. Make sure you have all your content details set up, for example, your email, telephone number, and website address.

There is the option to have a shop feature on a business page. You can showcase your products or services directly on your page. Making it easy for customers to buy from you could increase your sales by providing a hassle-free shopping experience.

Your page also has call-to-action (CTA) buttons. These are key! They get visitors to 'Shop now', 'Contact Us', or 'Sign Up', leading to more engagement and valuable conversations that can truly boost your business.

Consistency is key with Facebook business pages—I recommend you post every day. Keep your audience interested by mixing it up, use the 4:1 ratio as I mentioned earlier.

CHAPTER 6

The Power of Facebook Groups

My favourite topic to talk about is Facebook groups—I love groups!

An active group can be one of the biggest lead magnets for your business. It's where the party happens and where you can create the magic. Facebook groups allow you to drive meaningful interactions and build strong connections. Groups can foster genuine relationships and increase your brand visibility.

Did You Know ......
- Facebook has 3 billion active monthly users
- There are 1.7 billion Active users every month
- There are 10 million Facebook groups
- 1.8 billion people use Facebook groups every month
- The average Facebook User is in over 5 Facebook groups
- An engaged group can get anything from 50% - 80% of your members seeing your content versus a page that gets 3%-5%

Facebook has developed over the years and wants people to use the platform to create thriving online communities. It gives content in groups preferential treatment and pushes that content out to more people.

Facebook groups are powerful; they help people connect over shared interests or provide support and solutions to problems. They enable the group members to connect, engage, and support one another. Groups offer a platform for like-minded people to come together, exchange ideas and find a sense of belonging. When group members talk, share stories, and ask for help, groups turn into an exceptional place to gain knowledge and grow personally.

The fact is, people buy from people they know, like, and trust; a Facebook group is a perfect way to do that.

Let's start with the basics.

Setting up your Facebook Group
Group Name
Having the right name for your group is crucial.

Does the name make it easy to understand who the group is for and what it's all about? If it isn't clear, then people won't join, or you won't attract your ideal client.

Does your name have enough relevant Search Engine Optimised (SEO) words? Have as many SEO words in your title as possible. The key is knowing what your ideal client is likely to search for, so your group appears at the top of the search results.

You can change your group name every 28 days but, I don't recommend doing it that often.

Top Tip Hack
You can change the group name every 3 months by just adding an emoji. Facebook will notify all your group members, which will remind them about the group.

Header Image
Don't forget to add a header image to your group, just like you did for your profile and page, to show what your group is all about. Your banner image is a great sales tool. Use it to promote something every month! Remember, your banner image is one of the first things people see when they drop into your group or check in.

I use my banners to promote something different each month in what I want to drive people's intention too. That could be something for sale, a challenge or a free lead magnet.

Group Settings
Set your group settings to private and visible.

Why?
Your group, your rules. Making it private gives you more control over who can join and see the content. The approved members are the only ones who can access and take part in your group. Privacy is key to keeping out unwanted guests or troublemakers in your community.

A private group also encourages a more engaged community. Members are more likely to share openly and interact with each other when they feel comfortable in a safe and trusted space. The private setting can also create a sense of exclusivity, making members feel valued and part of a select community.

Don't forget to set your private group as visible so others can find and join it.

Joining Questions
Don't forget to set up joining questions for your group. You or any other admin can screen and approve new members. Ask the right questions to make sure new members are a good fit for the group. These questions can help you spot and block bots, spammers, and fake accounts trying to join.

Quick Tip
I'd think twice before adding someone who's new to Facebook to the group. If they just got on Facebook in the last few months, I'm not likely to approve.

You can use questions as a marketing tool and gather useful information from members.

These are the three questions I ask new members to join my group and why I have them.

Question 1
Drop your email address below and I will send you the link to download my ten top tips to grow your Facebook group. (This gives me permission to pop you onto our mailing list. You will only receive freebies, top tips, and any offers.)

Remember, we don't own our social media audience. They can take away our access to any of the platforms or our accounts from us. Therefore, this question helps me grow my email list. Once you approve access to your group and are on your mailing list, they become your warm market and much easier to convert into purchasing from you.

If you haven't started an email list yet, I highly recommend doing so. Make it the first thing you start after reading this book!

To help, I have a course 'Increasing your Email Subscribers: How to build a profitable email list and gain more subscribers every week.

Question 2
What's the biggest social media challenge you're facing with your business right now? Can I contact you to see how I can help?

I'm asking this question to know what my members need so that I can create the perfect content for my group.

I ask if they want me to contact them. If they say yes, I can DM them without it being spammy since they gave me permission.

Question 3
Where did you hear about us?

Finding out what marketing is working and what isn't helps me plan my strategy and make adjustments.

Unleashing Facebook Visibility

How are people finding my group? Is it in a Facebook search, personal recommendation, or from a networking meeting? I've been a guest speaker at an event and on a podcast. Has that exposure brought new people to my group? When you know what's working, you can do more of it.

So, asking these joining questions can help you in lots of ways.

Introduction Post
I always recommend having an introduction or welcome post pinned to the top of your group. Remember the saying "first impression count." A pinned post is often the first post new members see when joining a group.

A well-crafted welcome message can make new members feel appreciated and excited about joining the community.

Your welcome post should include important information about your group's purpose, rules, and announcements. This will help your new members understand what your group is about and how they can take part effectively.

The welcome post can introduce you as well. Share a little about yourself, business, group, and mission/values; build that rapport and help your members know, like, and trust you.

So Now Let's Talk Content ….
How to run and build an engaging Facebook group is a huge topic. Sadly, too immense for this book, however, I have a

core collection of courses that will teach you all about running a successful Facebook group.

A Facebook group is about building a community.

Think about what your members would want to see. Don't limit it to only what you can provide. Could you bring in guest experts to provide extra support to your members for other areas they may also need help with?

For example, in my group I give help and tips about social media, specifically, Facebook. But I know my members need help and support in other areas of their business, too. That's why I have guest experts give free masterclasses each month covering topics like branding, SEO, mindset, and marketing.

Have a think about what your ideal client may also need help with.

Quick Tips
- Post three times a day in your group
- Provide value
- Use tools like the guide feature
- Run polls, go lives and share reels
- Ask your members questions
- Reply to every comment where possible
- Show you and your personality

For suggestions about the type of content to post in your group, try a mixture of:

Discussions and Questions
Encourage group members to start discussions and ask questions related to the group's focus. This can spark meaningful conversations and interactions among members.

Tips and Advice
Share valuable tips, advice, or how-to guides related to the group's niche. Providing helpful information can position you as an authority in the field and keep members engaged.

News and Updates
Keep the group informed about the latest news, trends, or updates relevant to the group's interests.

Member Spotlights
Highlight the achievements, projects, or stories of group members. This fosters a sense of community and appreciation within the group.

Polls and Surveys
Conduct polls or surveys to gather feedback from members. This makes them feel involved and valued while also giving you information to help you create more content your audience wants to see.

Inspiring Quotes or Images
Share motivational quotes, images, or success stories related to the group's focus to uplift and inspire members.

Group Challenges or Events
Plan some fun challenges or events to get everyone involved and feel like part of the community.

Educational Resources
Share relevant articles, videos, or podcasts that can enhance members' knowledge and skills.

Announcements and Group Updates
Keep members informed about any changes, upcoming events, or important announcements related to the group.

Share Behind-The-Scenes
Don't forget how many people love reality TV. Our audience is interested in our lives, so don't be afraid to share some insider info to make them feel closer to you.

How Often Should You Post in Your Group?
I recommend posting no more than three times a day in your group.

Remember My 4:1 Ratio.
When planning your content, 80% should be a variety of the above examples. But don't forget that 20% should be sales posts—your group's there to earn you money, after all.

I'm very passionate about Facebook groups and have a lot to say about the subject, as you may have guessed. However, I'm going to leave groups parked here for now and move onto the next topic. The Five Pillars of Content.

CHAPTER 7

Content Foundations: The Five Pillars To Capture Attention

Have you ever wondered why people flock to social media platforms like Facebook, Instagram, and TikTok?

As business owners, we need to know the five big reasons people use social media to make content that really hits its target. These are called the five pillars. Each pillar serves as a cornerstone for crafting engaging and valuable social media posts.

But wait, there's something you've got to know before we start. To make your content stand out, you've got to know your audience better than you know yourself. To get it right, you need to know their needs, what annoys them, what they prefer, and what they aspire to. If you know what they worry about and what motivates them, you can make your content more valuable and relatable.

Let's explore the

Five Pillars of Content

Pillar 1 – Entertainment
One of the main reasons people turn to social media is to be entertained. They want to find content that brings a smile to their faces, makes them laugh, or uplifts their spirits. Embrace this aspect and create content that sparks joy and amusement.

Engaging content ideas for this pillar includes:

Funny Memes
Spread some humour with industry-related memes

Positive Quotes
Inspire and motivate your audience with uplifting quotes

Bloopers/Outtakes
Show the real and human side of your business with some bloopers and outtakes

Funny Stories
Share any hilarious incidents that have happened to you or your team

Witty Observations
Don't be afraid to be funny - sprinkle some humour into your industry-related content

Interactive Quizzes and Challenges
Engage your audience with fun quizzes and challenges that reflect your brand

Caption Contests
Post a photo and encourage your audience to come up with creative captions

Pillar 2 – Inspiration/Motivation

People scroll through social media to get inspired and motivated, hunting for content that resonates with their dreams and pumps them up.

Here are some ideas to add inspiration to your content strategy:

Quotes and Affirmations
Share powerful quotes and affirmations that uplift and inspire your audience

Success Stories
Highlight success stories, whether they are your own achievements or those of your clients

Lessons Learned
Share valuable lessons you've learned on your entrepreneurial journey

Personal Development
Discuss personal development activities or books that have positively affected your life

Admirable Figures
Give a shout-out to people who inspire you or others in your field and explain why they're so amazing

Pillar 3 – Education
Social media users crave knowledge and value informative content that teaches them something new. Position yourself as an authority in your field and educate your audience.

Here are some content ideas:

Share Your Knowledge
Share your expertise on topics that apply to your audience

Tips and Hacks
Share your best practical advice to help your audience overcome common problems

Mini Courses
Create bite-sized courses or tutorials that deliver valuable knowledge

Blogs and Webinars
Keep your audience engaged by writing blogs and hosting webinars on topics that interest them

Guest Appearances
Share your expertise as a guest in other groups, on podcasts, blogs, or publications

Pillar 4 – Connection
Social media is all about making and keeping connections. Use some strategies to encourage your audience to take part and get them involved.

Here are some ideas you can incorporate into your content:

Engagement Posts
Make posts that get people talking

Q&A Sessions
Have sessions where you answer questions and concerns from your followers

Surveys and Polls
Ask your audience for their thoughts and opinions with regular surveys and polls

Respond to Comments
Interact with your audience by replying to comments and sparking conversations

Facebook Visibility
Facebook loves active users, so the more you talk, the more they'll show your stuff

Pillar 5 – Convince/Promotion

As a business owner, your ultimate goal is to persuade your audience that they can't live without your product or service. You need to be strategic when promoting, always thinking of what your audience wants.

Some effective approaches include:

Identify Pain-Points
What's causing your client trouble? Understand your ideal clients' frustrations, needs, and desires, then address them in your content

Solutions-Oriented Content
In other words, content that helps solve problems. Show your audience how your product/service can fix their problems and fulfil their desires

Customer-Centric Approach
Forget about your business for a moment and think about how you can best serve your audience. Shift the focus from your business to your audience's needs and how you can serve them effectively

So, that's it, are you currently incorporating these Five Pillars of Content into your social media strategy?

If you do, you'll have a balance of interesting posts that your followers will love, engage with, and connect to for a long time.

Don't forget, knowing your audience is everything. Tailor your content to bring value, resonate with them, and establish your brand as a trusted source in your niche.

Embrace these pillars, and you'll be well on your way to harnessing the full potential of social media for your business.

CHAPTER 8

Spinning Success: Crafting Your Content Wheel

If you want to get ahead in the ever-changing world of social media, let me share a secret weapon with you – the Content Wheel!

This nifty tool will become your go-to guide in creating interesting content that speaks directly to your target audience. So, the next time you're feeling stuck on what to post, fret not; the Content Wheel will come to your rescue!

Here's How to Create a Content Wheel

You have a blank piece of paper in front of you, and in the centre, draw a small circle. In that circle, write your job title and the specific group of people you serve. This core represents your niche and is the heart of your content strategy.

From this central point, create a spider diagram by extending at least four arrows in different directions. At the end of each arrow, jot down a problem or issue your ideal clients commonly face.

Now create posts that solve these problems.

It's remarkable how you can come up with over 20 unique challenges your clients might encounter! That's enough for an entire month.

Example of My Content Wheel

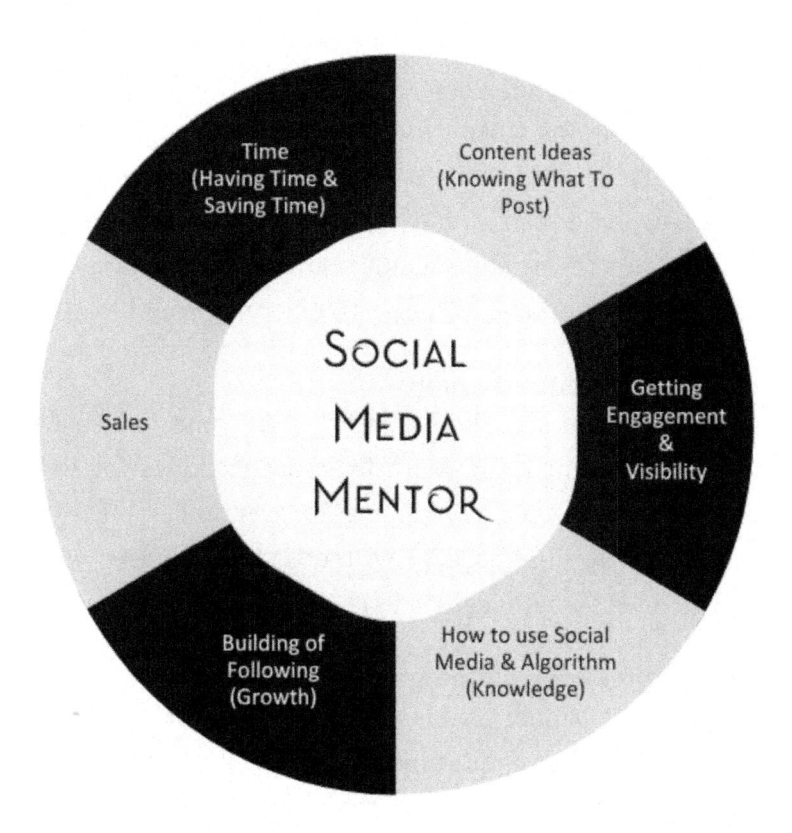

Social Media Mentor content wheel segments:
- Time (Having Time & Saving Time)
- Content Ideas (Knowing What To Post)
- Getting Engagement & Visibility
- How to use Social Media & Algorithm (Knowledge)
- Building of Following (Growth)
- Sales

Benefits of the Content Wheel

Now, let's delve into why creating this visual mind map, the Content Wheel, is incredibly helpful for your content creation process:

Visualisation Sparks Creativity

As humans, we are wired to think visually. Drawing your ideas on paper engages a distinct part of your brain. It helps you visualise connections between your job title, target audience, and their challenges. This process sparks creativity and opens up new pathways for content ideas.

Focus on Your Audience
With the Content Wheel, you keep your target audience at the centre of your content strategy. By identifying *their* problems, you can create content that is specifically tailored to address their needs and concerns. This is how you establish yourself as the go-to person in your niche.

Endless Content Possibilities
Once your Content Wheel is ready, it becomes a treasure trove of content ideas. With five content ideas for each problem, you'll have a whopping 20 outstanding pieces of content at your disposal. This method guarantees you'll always have something new to share.

Consistency and Planning
The Content Wheel enables you to plan your content in advance. Creating a monthly content calendar is easy with 20 content pieces. The more organised you are, the more consistent your posting schedule will be. It also helps you stay in line with your content strategy.

Tailored Solutions
Offering solutions for your audience's problems gives them useful ideas and steps to take. Your audience will appreciate the practical insights you offer, which can strengthen the bond between you and your followers.

Efficient Content Creation
The Content Wheel streamlines your content creation process. Instead of staring at a blank screen, wondering what to write about, you can simply refer to your wheel and choose the next content topic. This efficiency gives you more time to focus on other parts of your business.

Versatility Across Platforms
The beauty of the Content Wheel lies in its versatility. You can use your ideas on different platforms, like social media, blogs, podcasts, videos, and more. You can repurpose content while keeping it relevant to your audience's preferences on each platform.

Navigating Trends and Changes
What's hot on social media and what people like changes quickly. The Content Wheel is a flexible tool that helps you adjust your content strategy to keep up with trends and tackle fresh issues.

So, Your Homework Is to Create Your Content Wheel.
Take some time to think deeply about your job title, the people you serve, and the challenges they encounter.

Draw your wheel, identify those problems, and brainstorm five content ideas for each.

You'll soon find yourself armed with a month's worth of engaging content – one outstanding piece for each weekday.

Remember, the Content Wheel is your roadmap. It can help you captivate your audience and forge meaningful connections. Embrace it, and watch your social media presence soar!

Happy content creating!

CHAPTER 9

Content that Converts: Navigating Your Buyer's Journey

Before we dive into creating content that sells like hotcakes, let's set the foundation by understanding your buyer's journey.

It's like mapping out a thrilling adventure for your audience. Guiding them from the moment they realise they have a problem or need to the triumphant decision of choosing your solution.

Most people go through three stages when they buy something. For every stage, we need to tweak content to cater to your audience's changing needs and worries.

Stage 1: Awareness
Your audience knows they need help and begins searching for solutions. Sometimes, it's your content that triggers this awareness, making them realise they might need your "thing."

Get people interested by using educational posts, blogs, informative videos, reels, or live sessions.

Remember, this stage is about providing valuable information and establishing your authority in the field.

Stage 2: Consideration

Your audience is currently checking out different options and looking for more detailed information on possible solutions.

Content tailored for the consideration stage should delve into the nitty-gritty. Reel them in with content like in-depth guides, masterclasses, and some inspiring case studies and testimonials.

This stage is all about demonstrating why your product or service is the best choice.

Stage 3: Decision

At last, your audience is ready to decide and choose a solution that resonates with them.

Content for the decision stage should emphasise the benefits of your product or service. Showcase how it effectively meets their needs. And, of course, don't forget to include an irresistible CTA to encourage them to take the next step.

You now understand the three stages a buyer goes through and what content is best.

Here are four key questions to ask yourself when creating content.

1. What Does Your Product or Service Do for Your Client?
   How does your product/service benefit your clients?

Think about what they need and want, and show them how it solves their problems.

2. What Problems Does It Solve?
   Identify the frustrations your audience faces. Let them know that your product/service is the hero they need.

3. What Needs Does Your Product or Service Satisfy?
   Understand the specific needs of your target audience. Show how your solution perfectly caters to those needs.

4. How Does What You Provide Improve Your Ideal Client's Life?
   Paint a vivid picture of the positive impact your product or service will have on their lives. Make them envision a better version of themselves with your help.

If you answer these questions in your content, you'll attract your ideal client and connect with them for real.

Remember, every piece of content should have a purpose and align with your audience's interests and preferences.

Here are ten effective ways to create content that converts and engages your audience:

1. Keep it short & sweet
   People have notoriously short attention spans on social media. Aim for content between 100-250 characters, as studies show it gains more engagement.

Unleashing Facebook Visibility

2. Use graphics/photos with faces
   Human faces capture attention and evoke emotions. Share selfies or images featuring you and your clients to humanise your brand.

3. Grab attention with standout graphics
   Blurry or pixelated graphics won't cut it. Make sure your visuals are bold, captivating, and grab attention at first glance.

4. Be clear about your content's purpose
   Every post should serve a purpose. Whether it's to educate, entertain, or inspire, know what you want to achieve with each post.

5. Speak your audience's language
   Use language that resonates with your ideal client, using words and phrases they can relate to.

6. Hookline and CTA
   Every post should have a hook to grab attention and a strong CTA to get your audience to take the desired action.

7. Connect through storytelling
   Storytelling is a powerful tool to engage your audience emotionally. Share your journey, your successes, and your challenges. Make your brand relatable.

8. Involve your audience in your journey
   Take your audience on your entrepreneurial journey with you. Share your highs and lows, your goals, and your passion. People love being part of the journey and will support you along the way.

9. Timing matters
   Adjust your posting schedule based on when your target audience is online. Keep in mind things like hot weather or holiday season that could affect your reach.

10. Engage through questions and interactive posts
    Encourage conversations with your audience by asking questions and creating interactive posts. People love to share their thoughts and opinions.

By using these strategies in your content creation process, you'll raise your social media game. You'll also connect with your audience on a deeper level and transform leads into loyal customers.

Keep in mind that creating content that converts relies on understanding your audience, telling your story, and giving real value.

So, get ready to conquer your buyer's journey and create content that leaves a lasting impact!

Happy content crafting!

CHAPTER 10

Hooklines & CTAs: Captivate and Compel

In the past-paced arena of social media content, attention spans are short. Your content's success hinges on how well you master the art of the hookline and the CTA. These two powerhouses can help you grab your audience's attention, drive engagement, and motivate them to take meaningful action.

Let's see how they work and use them to your advantage.

Hooklines: The Spark That Ignites Engagement
Imagine a crowded room where everyone is speaking at once.

Amidst the chaos, your hookline is the voice that rises above the noise, capturing attention and inviting people to listen.

So, What Exactly Is a Hookline?
A hookline is a compact, attention-grabbing statement or headline. Think of it as your content's front door.

Why Are Hooklines so Crucial?
Attention Snagging
Your hookline is your virtual handshake, your chance to introduce yourself to the world. In a matter of seconds, it can determine whether your content is worth exploring further.

Shareability Magnet
A well-crafted hookline is like a magnetic force that compels your audience to share your content. If your hookline strikes a chord, your reach can expand exponentially as people share your content with their networks.

First Impressions Matter
The initial impression your content makes is often irreversible. A strong hookline ensures you start on the right foot and entice your audience to keep reading.

Consider this: eight out of ten people will read your headline, but only two out of ten will read the rest of your content. This highlights the pivotal role of your hookline in stopping the scroll.

Here are some captivating hookline examples to add to your toolkit:

- Discover the Secret to Banishing [Insert Problem].
- 10 Life-Changing Tips for Embracing [Insert Aspirational Lifestyle].
- Warning: This [Insert Product or Service] Could Revolutionise Your Life!
- The Ultimate Guide to Conquering [Insert Pain-Point].
- Are You Guilty of These Common Mistakes?
- Bid Farewell to [Insert Common Problem] Forever.
- The Surprising Truth Behind [Insert Myth Busted Wide Open]!

- Unveiling the Hidden Realities of [Insert Industry Fact]!

CTAs: The Compass of Engagement

That's just the beginning! You've got to keep the momentum going after your audience is hooked. You need a guiding force that directs your audience's next steps. This is where the CTA comes into play.

CTAs are like a light bulb that turns passive people into active ones. Without a well-crafted CTA, your audience may simply scroll on by, missing out on opportunities to engage with your content.

What's the Magic Behind CTAs?

Driving Engagement
CTAs prompt your audience to interact, encouraging them to like, comment, share, or take other desired actions. They're the bridge between passive consumption and active engagement.

Navigating Action
Just as a GPS guides you to your destination, a CTA guides your audience towards what you want them to do next. Whether it's signing up for a newsletter, clicking a link, or making a purchase, a strong CTA influences their choices.

Creating Urgency
Crafting a sense of urgency can motivate quick actions. Phrases like "limited time offer, grab it now" or "act now"

trigger a fear of missing out (FOMO), driving timely decisions.

Consider this: Emails with a single CTA increased clicks by 371% and sales by 1617%, according to a study by WordStream.

Here are some CTA examples that guide your audience's interactions:

- Secure Your Spot for Our Upcoming Free Webinar – Book Now!
- Unlock Expert Advice on [Insert Topic] – Schedule a Call Today.
- Limited Time Offer – Shop Now Before It's Gone!
- Show Your Agreement: Like this Post.
- Join the Conversation: Share Your Thoughts in the Comments.
- Which Top Tip Resonates with You? Let Us Know!
- Express Connection: Drop a Heart if You Relate.
- Ignite Your Creativity: Caption This Post.
- Speak Up: Do You Agree or Disagree?
- Engage: Have You Ever Done This? Share Your Experience.
- Make Your Choice: Vote A or B.
- Stay Updated: Follow Us for More Exciting Content.
- Dive Deeper: Click the Link in the Bio.
- Share Your Emotion: Drop Your Favourite Emoji Below.

- Unlock Access: Get Unlimited Benefits by Following [Insert Instruction].

Crafting Effective CTAs: Top Tips

Strong Verbs
Start your CTA with powerful action verbs that spur your audience into motion.

Emotion and Enthusiasm
Infuse emotion and enthusiasm to make your CTA more interesting and irresistible.

Reasons to Act
Clearly state the benefits your audience will gain by taking the desired action.

FOMO Leveraging
Utilise FOMO by emphasising the limited availability or exclusivity of the opportunity.

The Dynamic Duo

Hooklines and CTAs are a dynamic duo that shape your content's destiny. The hookline grabs attention, while the CTA guides it purposefully. They are your allies in standing out, building engagement, and driving conversions. So, make sure you put some thought into it, try different things, and remember how much it affects your social media success. With the right hookline and CTA, you'll hook your audience and inspire them to take action that aligns with your brand's mission.

In the end, it's all about forging connections, sparking conversations, and building a community that thrives on shared value. Integrate these tools into your content strategy today. See your social media game get stronger. Start to really connect with your audience, turn leads into sales, and make a lasting impact.

It's time to harness the magic of hooklines and CTAs – your content's secret weapons.

CHAPTER 11

The Art of Storytelling: Building Bonds Through Connection

At the heart of every successful business lies a fundamental truth: connection is key.

Throughout the book, we've explored ways to connect with your audience, build trust, and make your business thrive. Treat your customers well and they'll be back for more. Plus, they'll tell their friends.

We're in a digital age, and people don't meet as often as they used to. That's why storytelling is so powerful. It helps us connect beyond screens and wires.

The Power of Storytelling: Forging Bonds that Last
Storytelling is about more than just relaying information. It's like bringing your audience into your world and sharing a story that they can relate to. We all feel the same emotions and it makes us feel connected. When you share your story, you invite your audience to relate, empathise, and invest emotionally in your journey.

Why Storytelling? The Science Behind It
The science behind storytelling is remarkable.

Studies show that stories affect your brain in a big way. When we hear stories, our brain not only understands the language but also imagines the complete scene. This phenomenon is often referred to as neural coupling. Put simply, it creates a shared experience between the storyteller and the listener, fostering deeper connections.

Content Ideas: Crafting Your Narrative
So, how can you harness the power of storytelling in your content strategy? Here are some content ideas to blend your narrative with your brand.

1. Your Starter Story
   Share the roots of your business – how it all began. Did a personal experience trigger the idea? Was there a pivotal moment that ignited your entrepreneurial journey?

2. Introduce Yourself
   Peel back the layers and let your audience know who you are. What shaped you? What experiences moulded your perspective and led you to where you are today?

3. Childhood Dreams
   Connect the dots between your childhood aspirations and your current business. Did your childhood dreams mirror the path you're now treading?

4. Inspirations
   Reveal the sources of your inspiration. Was it a book, a mentor, a life event? Sharing your influencers humanises your journey.

5. Morning Rituals
   Offer a glimpse into your daily routine. Morning rituals, in particular, can provide insight into your mindset and set the tone for the day.

6. Hobbies & Interests
   You're not just a business; you're a multifaceted individual. Share your hobbies, passions, and interests beyond the business realm.

7. Shout Outs
   Who are the businesses that inspire you? Give them some recognition. This isn't just about being nice, it shows you're part of the community.

8. Me Time
   Balancing work and personal life is an ongoing challenge. Discuss how you carve out "me time" to rejuvenate and recharge.

9. Life Updates
   Believe it or not, your audience takes an interest in your life beyond business. Keep them updated on your adventures add milestones.

10. Self-Improvement
    Share about how you've been developing yourself and your company. Whether you're learning something new or going to a life-changing seminar, sharing your journey makes you more relatable.

11. First Customer
    Take your audience back to your humble beginnings — your first-ever customer or sale. Relive the emotions and lessons from that milestone.

12. Successes Beyond Work
    Success isn't confined to business achievements. Share some personal successes that show all the different sides of you.

13. Words of Wisdom
    Discuss quotes, books, or ideas that inspire you. It's a way to invite your audience into your thought processes and values.

14. Mission & Values
    Unearth the mission and values that drive your business. When your audience understands your purpose, they're more likely to align with your brand.

15. Behind-the-Scenes
    Offer a backstage pass to your daily activities. Showcase your workspace, your team, and the magic that happens behind-the-scenes.

16. Customer Success Stories
    Can you share some stories about your satisfied customers' transformative experiences? People relate

better to real-life examples that show the practical benefits of what you offer.

The Widespread Impact: Why Storytelling Works

Storytelling has become a cornerstone of modern marketing for several compelling reasons:

Authenticity

In a world dominated by polished ads, stories offer authenticity. They showcase the journey, the ups and the downs, making your brand relatable and genuine.

Emotional Engagement

Stories evoke emotions, and emotions drive decisions. By creating an emotional connection, you tap into a powerful avenue for influencing behaviour.

Retention and Recall

Stories are easier to remember than facts for us humans. A well-told tale can make your brand more memorable.

Differentiation

Your story is unique. In a crowded market, your narrative can set you apart, helping you stand out amidst the noise.

Examples of Effective Storytelling in Marketing

Nike

Nike's iconic slogan "Just Do It" is more than a tagline. This is a CTA inspired by a guy with cerebral palsy who didn't let his condition define him. People really connect with this. It's more than just shoes - it represents empowerment.

Coca-Cola
Coke's holiday ads with polar bears make you feel all warm and fuzzy inside and stoke up the festive spirit. These heartwarming stories invoke emotional connections with the brand.

Apple
Apple believes their products can help you on your personal journey to success. These stories make the brand's offerings more relatable and desirable.

In the digital age, storytelling isn't just a strategy; it's a necessity. Face-to-face chats are rare, but stories can make your brand more human and trustworthy. Plus, they'll keep your customers loyal. When you tell a story, you're sharing more than just facts, you're encouraging a connection. When you blend your story with your brand, you create a meaningful connection that goes beyond the digital world.

Your Narrative, Your Legacy

Don't forget that every story you tell is more than just content. You're creating a legacy that speaks to your audience, builds trust, and sets you apart in the market. Through storytelling, you're not just selling products or services; you're selling experiences, emotions, and values.

Make sure your content is not just informative but also transformative by telling a story. Your story isn't just a chapter; it's the essence of your brand.

CHAPTER 12

Embracing Authenticity: Forging Genuine Connections

In this digital world, where screens rule our lives, it's weird that we still want real human connections. People look for stories that resonate on a personal level, experiences that go beyond the virtual realm.

"Get To Know Me" content isn't just about unveiling the person behind the brand. It's about creating a bridge that spans the gap between the digital and the real, building trust, loyalty, and lasting relationships.

The Power of Personal Connection: Going Beyond Products

As covered in the storytelling chapter, your audience wants more than just transactions. They want to know the person shaping the brand, the narratives that colour your life, the experiences that mould your perspective.

Lifestyle posts have a special kind of magic to them. They make you feel you're talking to a friend, even online.

Data Speaks: The Influence of Personal Stories

Did you know lifestyle posts have higher engagement on social media? That's across every platform, not just Facebook.

This trend highlights the importance of human connections in a data-driven world. These posts offer more than a mere glance into your world; they beckon your audience to take part, react, and engage on a personal level.

If you want to succeed in a world ruled by algorithms, you need to focus on engagement. And "Get To Know Me" content is how you do it.

Embracing Vulnerability: Seamlessly Infusing Personal Stories

Imagine peeling back the layers of the corporate veneer and allowing your audience a glimpse of the person steering the ship. That's the essence of "Get To Know Me" content.

Building a genuine connection requires being vulnerable. Be real with your audience and share both the good and bad.

Don't just focus on business transactions invite your audience into your world and you'll create a genuine connection that lasts.

Here are some examples of posts you could create to build that rapport.

Home Life
Introduce your inner circle – family and pets. The warmth of these relationships invites your audience to connect on a personal level.

Unleashing Facebook Visibility

Global Footprints
Share your journey around the world. Each home holds a story that means something.

Furry Companions
Let's face it, adorable animals are universal crowd-pleasers. Introducing your pets lets your audience see a softer side of your brand.

Culinary Chronicles
Food is like a universal language. When you talk about your food likes and share your food stories, you connect over similar experiences.

Adventures in Leisure:
Let's see your personal adventures - holiday snaps, day trips, and hobbies. These moments add a human touch to your brand.

Interactive Q&A
Open the floor to audience questions. This is how you make your brand more relatable and get people excited to engage.

Wisdom from Experience
Offer nuggets of wisdom you've gained on your journey. Sharing personal insights adds value and depth to your brand.

The Face Behind the Brand
A selfie isn't just a picture; it's an invitation into your world. Taking selfies helps people see your brand as friendly and easy to relate to.

Literary Escapes
Books are windows to the soul. Or so my editor tells me. Lol! Share what you're currently reading. Discussing the impact it has on you can lead to thought-provoking conversations with fellow book lovers.

Entertainment Enthusiast
What TV shows, movies, or documentaries are you loving right now? Open up the discussions, chat and connect!

Celebrating Others
Show some love to other businesses and accounts that you like. It's a way to show what you're interested in and build community spirit.

Trials to Triumphs
Share your struggles, and how you've overcome them. Opening up and being vulnerable helps us create a shared narrative.

Cheers to Achievements
Don't hold back on sharing your successes, milestones, and moments to celebrate. Let your audience celebrate your victories with you.

Humour as a Bond
Laughter unites us all. Sharing a funny anecdote creates an immediate connection, making the virtual feel more personal.

Dreams Unveiled
Reveal your aspirations and dreams. Your audience could feel the same with shared ambitions, leading to meaningful conversations.

Messages to Our Past
This is fun. Craft a message to your younger self, sharing insights and wisdom garnered from your journey. "Hey, little me! Here are some things I wish I knew earlier. "

The Psychology of Connection: The Power of Authenticity

Reality TV, personal blogs, and vlogs didn't just happen by chance. It's a basic truth that people are interested in others and want to understand them!

Psychologists have a theory called the "mere exposure effect" that explains this. According to the theory, the more you see something or someone, the more you prefer it/them.

Your "Get To Know Me" content takes advantage of this human condition, creating familiarity that ultimately builds trust.

Respecting Boundaries: Sharing Safely
Sharing personal information on the internet can be intimidating — I understand that.

Always remember that you have the power to choose what to share. You don't have to divulge everything; in fact, setting boundaries is healthy. Share what feels right for you and align with your brand's values.

Nowadays, people share too much. Being authentic doesn't mean telling everything, but sharing honestly.

Crafting Bonds Through Authenticity

When you add "Get To Know Me" content to your brand, don't forget that each post is a chance to connect with your audience.

Your stories are the threads that make up your brand's story and bring you and your audience closer together, even beyond the internet. These little details make a community that doesn't just watch but joins in on your journey.

Business is more about relationships than transactions. When you embrace the personal touch, you'll see people go from passive to passionate. Every time you post, you're not just telling stories - you're asking your followers to join in and become part of the story. Your brand wouldn't be complete without them.

CHAPTER 13

Elevate Your Audience: The Power of Helping

"We rise by lifting others. "

~ Robert Ingersoll.

It's totally true that in business, we climb higher by lifting others. Helping your audience can be a great way to build a stronger relationship with them, even if it seems counterintuitive. When you offer real help related to your business, you build a stronger connection and become a valuable resource.

In this chapter, we'll explore the psychology behind this approach and how to use it in your content strategy.

The Psychology of Help: Nurturing Trust and Connection

When you help someone, it can make a big difference in how they feel and how much they trust you. When you offer help, you're fulfilling a basic human desire for solutions and support.

When you offer this, you're not just marketing your products or services. You're showing a commitment to your audience's well-being.

This genuineness resonates, forming the bedrock of trust that modern businesses thrive upon.

Content Ideas That Forge Bonds
Here's the beauty of this strategy: not only does it enhance your audience's experience, but it's also a pathway to organic brand growth.

Let's explore these content ideas and the reasons they resonate so effectively:

How-To Guides
Share your expertise by creating how-to guides or videos. It speaks directly to what your audience wants and makes you the go-to person. This type of content shows you're an expert and teaches at the same time.

Voucher Tagging
Encourage your audience to tag someone who they think would like a voucher for your product or service. This idea gets people talking, shows how generous you are, and helps spread the word about your brand naturally.

Niche Insights
Give your audience what they want by sharing niche tips. Your industry knowledge in this content is valuable and establishes you as a leader.

Customer Stories
Highlighting a customer's journey creates a personal touch. This doesn't just boost their business, but it also shows off how great your products/services are, making your brand's worth more tangible.

Audience Input
The more you ask your audience what they need, the stronger your engagement becomes. Addressing concerns shows you care and brings the community together.

Motivational Posts
Everyone can relate to motivation. Posting motivational content lifts your audience up and shows your brand is all about positivity, not just business.

Organisational Tips:
Getting your followers organised can help in both personal and professional areas. It proves you care about improving their lives, not just selling to them.

Educational Initiatives
By creating a course or masterclass, you can increase the value you give to your audience. Sharing what you know helps you build trust as an educator, not just a business owner.

Gratitude Through Giveaways
Hosting a giveaway is a great way to say "thanks" to your followers and encourage them to give back. Collaborating with other businesses gets your brand out there, increasing your visibility and reach.

Guest Takeovers
Handing over your social media to another business owner for a day injects some fresh ideas. This cross-promotion helps both businesses and gets you more exposure.

Self-Improvement Recommendations
Sharing your top self-improvement book choices adds a personal touch. You're showing your dedication to personal growth and giving some valuable suggestions, too.

Charitable Events
Want to show you care? Host a charity event with your products or services. This is perfect for your socially conscious consumers.

Solution-Driven Posts
When you can identify common problems your customers have and fix them, it shows you're great at problem-solving. This not only helps but also makes you a trusted partner.

App Recommendations
Who doesn't love a good app? In a world full of tech, sharing your go-to apps helps your audience out. This makes you even more valuable.

Timesaving Tips
Work smarter instead of harder, right? Timesaving tips are a hit with everyone. Everybody's on the hunt for efficiency, so make your content relatable and easy to put into action.

Examples from Big Business
Leading companies understand the power of help-based content.

For instance, Apple's "Today at Apple" sessions offer free workshops on creative skills and software. These sessions engage users and showcase the brand's commitment to empowering customers.

Another notable example is HubSpot's Marketing Academy. They provide a wealth of free educational content, ranging from courses to certifications. This not only enhances their brand's value but also positions HubSpot as an authority in the marketing industry.

Advancing by Assistance

To sum up, helping others isn't just about giving aid - it's about creating trust, making connections, and building a community. When you address your audience's needs, you not only make their lives better but also make your brand look reliable and valuable.

The psychology behind this is simple - everyone wants support and solutions. The key to success when incorporating these content ideas into your plan is to stay authentic and genuine.

When you put in the work, your audience will show you love and become your biggest cheerleaders, telling others about your business.

CHAPTER 14

Value Beyond Measure: Building Lasting Relationships

In today's digital world, everyone is fighting for your attention. Step into the world of value-packed content. Businesses thrive when giving helpful solutions, insights, and guidance instead of just pushing sales.

If you focus on delivering value, you'll build a tribe of loyal followers who see your business as an expert and trust it.

This chapter talks about why this strategy works. I'll show you how it can lead to business growth and give you some creative tips for adding it to your content plan.

Value-Driven Content: The Psychology of Trust and Connection

The value-driven content strategy is all about giving back — what goes around comes around! Basically, if you give to others, they'll probably give back. You know this is true, because it's something you've done yourself.

When you offer your insights, knowledge, or resources, you're starting something positive. An engaged conversation. If your audience feels grateful for your value, they'll want to chat, take part, and maybe even buy from you.

Unleashing Facebook Visibility

Trust is the key to long-lasting relationships.

Content Ideas That Speak Volumes

This strategy is brilliant because it's so versatile and appeals to everyone.

These ideas really connect with all kinds of audiences. Ideas are valuable when they meet needs, provide insights, or offer solutions.

Sharing Success Stories

Talk about your personal successes and the journey it took to achieve them. This offers motivation and practical insights, inspiring your audience to strive for their goals.

Peek Behind the Curtain

Share behind-the-scenes videos or photos showcasing your products or services. Being honest makes us more real and helps grow a more genuine connection to our audience.

Promote Others' Stories

Highlight someone else's inspiring journey. This not only adds value to your content but also shows your willingness to celebrate others' achievements.

Audience Input

Ask your audience what content they'd like to see. This approach not only tailors your content to their needs but also empowers them, encouraging a sense of community.

Resource Recommendations
Discuss a product or service that has benefitted you within your niche. This will help boost your credibility as a knowledgeable resource.

Benefits Spotlight
Elaborate on the benefits of your products or services. This educates your audience on what you offer and helps them make informed decisions.

Face-to-Face Webinars
Host webinars to connect directly with your audience. This personal interaction deepens relationships and offers a platform for Q&A.

Knowledge-Centric Courses
Develop courses that work well with your products/services. This not only provides value but makes you an industry authority.

Lead Magnets
Offer freebies, like eBooks or PDFs, in exchange for signing up for your newsletter. By doing this, you'll grow your emails list and people get something they find useful.

Motivation Through Inspiration
Share your favourite motivational speakers or podcasts. By doing this, you provide value and show your audience you're dedicated to their personal growth, too.

Visual Demonstrations
Show people how to use your products with videos or reels. This adds a practical element to what you're offering.

Industry News Updates
What's the latest buzz in your industry or niche? This type of content proves you're on top of things and keeps your audience up-to-date.

Audience Check-Ins
Make sure to ask your audience about their well-being. It's the little things that make your followers feel like they're part of a community that cares.

Expert Interviews
Get some interviews with industry leaders. This adds credibility to your reputation and your audience will hear different perspectives.

Practical Tips and Hacks
Offer practical advice, tips, and life hacks that simplify your audience's daily life. You become someone people can count on.

Engaging Polls and Surveys
Make polls and surveys that people can interact with to get their feedback and opinions. It's not just about getting your audience engaged, it's also about tailoring your content.

Evidence from Industry Giants
Leading companies have recognised the potential of value-driven content.

Take Nike's "Nike Training Club" app that offers free workouts. This value establishes the company as a fitness authority and builds brand loyalty.

Similarly, social media scheduling tool, Buffer shares value-driven content with its blog. The blog has all the social media advice its audience needs. It's a valuable resource that drives traffic and makes Buffer a trusted source.

The Path to Connection and Growth
So, basically, value-driven content isn't just a strategy. It's more like a philosophy that helps build genuine relationships and grow your business.

By focusing on providing solutions, insights, and support, you're tapping into the psychology of reciprocity and trust. With this plan, your audience will be eager to engage, interact, and invest in what you're offering. Creating valuable content makes your audience love you more, turning them into your biggest fans.

> *Remember, in the realm of value,*
> *authenticity is the golden key.*

By using these content ideas, you're doing more than just solving your followers' problems. You're making a big difference and establishing your brand as a helpful guide for your audience.

CHAPTER 15

Celebrate and Connect: Nurturing Relationships Through Shared Joy

While professionalism is essential, injecting an element of fun into your content strategy can work wonders. It's not just about products and services; it's about forming genuine connections with your audience.

National and international days are the perfect time to bond with your followers.

So, in this chapter, we're going to check out how these celebration days match with the Five Pillars of Content and the buyer's journey. What's more significant is how they can establish meaningful dialogues and lasting connections.

Celebration Days: A Portal to Connection
These special days are more than just a chance to have fun; they're opportunities to form connections based on shared interests and values.

Use these special days to show who you really are, beyond your work persona.

When you take part in these days, you're inviting your audience to connect with you on a personal level.

Linking to the Five Pillars of Content

Remember the Five Pillars of Content we explored in chapter seven? You can use celebration days to support multiple pillars, so they're a great addition to your strategy.

Let me show you how:

1. Entertainment
   Celebration days add some light-heartedness and joy to your content, making your audience smile. It's all about making a positive bond.

2. Inspiration/Motivation
   These days are perfect for sharing stories of gratitude, triumph, and hope. When you celebrate your wins, it motivates others to chase their dreams.

3. Education
   Share the meaning behind each celebration day. Share the values, history, and customs of these days with your audience.

4. Connection
   Celebration days spark conversations. Bonding over similar interests and experiences nurtures a sense of connection in your community.

5. Convince/Promotion
   Make sure to chat with your audience, so it doesn't feel like you're just trying to sell them something.

Celebrating special days in your content is a great way to keep in line with the five pillars. This not only enriches your content but also deepens your bond with your audience. You're building rapport; a sense of relatability, trust, and engagement that lasts beyond the festivities.

Celebration Days and the Buyer's Journey

The buyer's journey is what we call the process people go through before buying something. I discussed it in chapter 9. It all boils down to three stages: awareness, consideration, and decision.

Want to hear a secret? You can strategically plan celebration days for each stage. Let me show you how:

Awareness Stage
Introduce celebration days that resonate with your audience's interests. This nurtures an initial connection, making them aware of your brand's values and personality.

Consideration Stage
Share personal stories or industry insights on relevant celebration days. Your brand looks like a source of inspiration and knowledge.

Decision Stage
Show how your products/services change lives by sharing customer stories on celebration days.

So, by adding celebration days to your content strategy, you can connect with your customers at every stage.

Yes, by strategically including celebration days, you're engaging your audience with captivating content. But there's more to it than that. You're also leading them through a full experience that fits their developing needs.

Content that celebrates is a valuable tool for connecting, building trust, and pushing your audience on their journey with your brand.

Crafting Celebration-Driven Content
Celebration days are a great opportunity to connect, share stories, and get emotion into the digital world.

These events make us happy and give brands a chance to make content that connects with their followers. Each celebration day is a chance to put some personality into your brand, connect for real, and create a community that loves sharing experiences.

Let's look at some celebration days and I'll share some potential content ideas:

Global Family Day (1st Jan)
Got any heartwarming family stories to share? Being relatable and authentic proves you're all about making genuine connections.

Unleashing Facebook Visibility

International Thank You Day (11th Jan)
Express gratitude to someone who's made a significant impact on your life. You'll have genuine interactions with your community through this.

World Thinking Day (22nd Feb)
Share an interesting fact or piece of knowledge related to your niche. Education and engagement go hand in hand.

International Women's Day (8th March)
Let's celebrate the outstanding achievements of some remarkable women in your industry or personal life! Your female audience will connect with this and it emphasises inclusivity.

World Book Day (22nd April)
Recommend a book that has influenced you. This not only offers value but also shows off your interests and values.

World Turtle Day (23rd May)
Who doesn't love turtles? Share a cute turtle-related image or fact. This content is all about having fun and spreading happiness.

International Chocolate Day (7th July)
Break the ice by asking about their favourite chocolate. This simple question makes people chat and shows your brand's human side.

International Friendship Day (1st August)
Give a shout-out to your friend or loyal customer. It's a nice way to say thank you and strengthen your community.

International Youth Day (12th August)
If it's applicable, brag about your kids or younger family members. Are there any achievements you can share? This sneak peek into your life is perfect for family-oriented people.

Never Give Up Day (18th August)
Take a moment to remember the tough moments and the moments of celebration on your journey. This motivational content will inspire your followers to keep going.

International Charity Day (5th Sept)
Offer a special promotion tied to a charity contribution. Your audience will love it and you're making a positive social impact.

World Gratitude Day (21st Sept)
Share what you're grateful for, encouraging your audience to reflect on their blessings, too.

World Smile Day (6th Oct)
Share a smiling selfie. This fun content spreads positivity and uplifts your audience. Smile and the entire world smiles with you.

World Mental Health Day (10th Oct)
Share self-care practices or a personal story. This will strike a chord with your audience's emotional well-being.

Winter Solstice (21st Dec)
Share what you love about winter. This type of content always gets people talking and feeling connected.

Unleashing Facebook Visibility

As you begin your journey of crafting celebration-focused content, get ready to find a world of opportunities to celebrate what matters. These moments bring us all together, no matter where we are or what we do.

Embracing these celebration days adds value and opens doors to wonderful conversations. When you open up and encourage others to do the same, you're building a sense of togetherness that goes beyond the virtual space.

Incorporating Celebration into Your Strategy - Crafting Moments of Connection
Don't wait! Start today. As you can see, using the power of celebration days can create lasting connections.

Craft content that aligns with your brand's values and personality. Engage your audience in conversations, inviting them to share their experiences and opinions.

Remember, when you include these celebration days into your content, you're not just promoting your business. You're building relationships that go beyond sales, creating a tribe that celebrates and sticks together. They'll be your biggest cheerleaders!

CHAPTER 16

Unleash Your Facebook Visibility Journey

You're now equipped with the tools and insights necessary to revamp your digital presence. With these strategies, you can create a strong online presence, connect with your ideal audience, and take your business to new heights.

Your journey doesn't end here, it's just the start. Social media is like a living thing that never stops changing. Be flexible and willing to adjust your strategies. Being able to change and adapt is what sets successful people apart in the digital world. Keep refining your approach on Facebook to stay ahead of the game.

Every time you post or connect, you can shape your story, show off your brand, and hook your audience. The canvas is huge, the inspiration rich, and the possibilities are boundless.

Remember that you're not alone on this journey. Community and collaboration are sparks for growth. If you're not already part of my vibrant Facebook community, I encourage you to join us. Share your victories, ask for guidance when challenges come up, and thrive in the camaraderie of fellow entrepreneurs on the same path.

Ready to level up your journey? Pink Fizz Social has got you covered.

Unleashing Facebook Visibility

- Dive into our low-cost membership programme — The Academy
- Explore personalised 1-1 mentoring
- Immerse yourself in transformative courses
- Undergo comprehensive audits of your digital strategy

Pink Fizz Social has the resources and guidance to speed up your success.

Remember, Facebook is more than just a platform. It's where you can paint your vision, share your story, and chase your dreams. Take what you learned from this book and dive into the endless possibilities of Facebook. Let it transform your business destiny!

Thanks for coming with me on this adventure. Don't stop expanding your digital footprint, leaving your mark on social media.

You got this!

Heather Rose

Founder, Pink Fizz Social

The Academy

Go from digital zero to marketing hero and boost your business with amazing courses and interactive posting.

We have all the right ingredients to help you get started straight away. Broaden your horizons with empowered training sessions.

Increase your confidence with coaching zoom calls and Q & A's

Build your business NOW and MAXIMISE your potential

Meet like-minded business owners helping each other

Be part of a dedicated support system of business owners

As a member you will enjoy special privileges

You'll be part of a select group of business owners all who share your passion for success!

For more Information visit https://pinkfizz.social/academy-cta

Or scan the following QR code and get your first month for £1

About the Author

Heather Rose - Your Guide to Elevating Your Business with Organic Facebook Marketing

Meet Heather Rose, the dynamic force propelling Pink Fizz Social to the forefront of the social media arena. Heather's a social media guru on a mission to help business owners dominate Facebook with organic marketing. She wants to help them get unparalleled visibility, engagement, and sales.

Heather's journey isn't just about strategies; it's a commitment to transforming your business. Her passion lies in gifting you the invaluable treasure of time freedom while forming a thriving online presence. Drawing from a wealth of social media wisdom, Heather navigates the intricate web of this ever-changing digital world with skill.

Her belief in the untapped potential of Facebook as a business catalyst is unwavering. Heather works closely with her clients to create strategies that match their goals and audience. This results in organic growth that feels authentic and rewarding.

Beyond the realm of numbers, Heather values the human pulse of social media. Her approach is all about making authentic connections, creating engagement, and driving business success.

Expect more than advice; anticipate a partnership that propels your aspirations. Heather's guidance is nuanced, her insights strategic, and her recommendations actionable. With her by your side, you'll master the labyrinth of social media marketing, armed with the tools and wisdom to flourish in the digital realm.

Heather Rose and Pink Fizz Social are the perfect team to help entrepreneurs and business owners alike grow their online presence.

Let's work together and unlock your business's full potential on Facebook. You'll see growth, visibility, and even have more time to do what you love.

Find Heather Online:

Website: https://pinkfizz.social
Email: info@pinkfizz.social

Group	https://www.facebook.com/groups/pinkfizzsocial
Page	https://www.facebook.com/pinkfizzsocial
LinkedIn	https://www.linkedin.com/in/heather-rose-0b11ab188/
TikTok	https://www.tiktok.com/@pinkfizz.social
Instagram	https://www.instagram.com/pinkfizzsocial

Acknowledgments

Huge thanks to my wonderful hubby Barry and my amazing dad, Xx. You're my biggest cheerleaders and always there for me.

My treasured mum in heaven, I know you're always with me, pushing me forward.

My beloved son, Isaac. You have been my inspiration ever since you were born. Thank you for saving me.

And finally, a big thanks to everyone who has bought this book. To all of you who are in my corner, cheering me on and supporting me. You're the reason I'm here, and I can't thank you enough.

A Special Thank You
This book wouldn't be the same without Kim Brockway's amazing expertise. Thank you! From editing to copywriting and everything in between. Kim's the one who made my scattered thoughts into this masterpiece.

If you need help with writing anything, Kim is the person you want. She's a real pro at crafting books, journals, ebooks, and even lead magnets.

She's the best at her craft and also one of the friendliest people you'll meet. Meeting with her is like a breath of fresh air, and her skills are amazing.

Kim won't let you down on your writing journey. You have my word.

Find Kim online here:

Facebook	https://www.facebook.com/kim.brockway.16
Twitter	https://twitter.com/KimProofreader
Instagram	https://www.instagram.com/kim.fictionedit
LinkedIn	https://www.linkedin.com/in/kim-brockway-0a72311b7/

Appendix 1

Table of Abbreviations

CRM   Customer Relationship Management
CTA   Call-to-action
FOMO Fear of missing out
SEO   Search Engine Optimised
DM   Direct Message

Your Notes

☆ Page 28-29
Put external links in Comments rather than the post itself
☆ try to change how words look or don't use as much eg. "Comment" / "Link" / "free" etc

☆ page 12 - reviews
"Community" is a facebook Buzz word

☆ Page 39
Setting your page up for success
- Links when people "click" on cover image (for personal page too)
- Simply add "click here" so people know to click the image, then add links

Heather Rose

Heather Rose

Unleashing Facebook Visibility

Heather Rose

Printed in Great Britain
by Amazon